LANDMARKS OF DEMOCRACY
AMERICAN INSTITUTIONS

ARLINGTON NATIONAL CEMETERY

AND THE TOMB OF THE UNKNOWN SOLDIER

JINNOW KHALID

PowerKiDS press
New York

Published in 2018 by The Rosen Publishing Group, Inc.
29 East 21st Street, New York, NY 10010

First Edition

Editor: Elizabeth Krajnik
Book Design: Reann Nye

Photo Credits: Cover Anton_Ivanov/Shutterstock.com; p. 4 robert cicchetti/Shutterstock.com; p. 5 Guillermo Olaizola/Shutterstock.com; pp. 6, 7 Everett Historical/Shutterstock.com; p. 9 Mark Wilson/Getty Images News/Getty Images; p. 10 https://commons.wikimedia.org/wiki/File:Montgomery_C_Meigs_grave_-_looking_S_detail_-_Arlington_National_Cemetery_-_2011.JPG; p. 11 https://commons.wikimedia.org/wiki/File:Montgomery_C._Meigs_-_Brady-Handy.jpg; p. 12 Joseph Sohm/Shutterstock.com; p. 13 Mark Reinstein/Corbis Historical/Getty Images; p. 15 fstockfoto/Shutterstock.com; p. 16 https://commons.wikimedia.org/wiki/File:TombUN.gif; p. 17 Cameron Davidson/The Image Bank/Getty Images; p. 18 Hugh Rooney/Eye Ubiquitous/Corbis Documentary/Getty Images; p. 19 Sergio TB/Shutterstock.com; p. 20 https://en.wikipedia.org/wiki/File:MichaelBlassie.jpg; p. 21 https://commons.wikimedia.org/wiki/File:Tomb_of_the_Unknowns_14.jpg; p. 23 Joseph M. Arseneau/Shutterstock.com.

Library of Congress Cataloging-in-Publication Data

Names: Khalid, Jinnow, author.
Title: Arlington National Cemetery and the Tomb of the Unknown Soldier / Jinnow Khalid.
Description: New York : PowerKids Press, 2018. | Series: Landmarks of democracy: American institutions | Includes index.
Identifiers: LCCN 2016056424| ISBN 9781508160939 (pbk. book) | ISBN 9781508160946 (6 pack) | ISBN 9781508160953 (library bound book)
Subjects: LCSH: Arlington National Cemetery (Arlington, Va.)–Juvenile literature. | Tomb of the Unknowns (Va.)–Juvenile literature. | Arlington (Va.)–Buildings, structures, etc.–Juvenile literature.
Classification: LCC F234.A7 K48 2018 | DDC 975.5/295–dc23
LC record available at https://lccn.loc.gov/2016056424

Manufactured in the United States of America

CPSIA Compliance Information: Batch #BS17PK: For Further Information contact Rosen Publishing, New York, New York at 1-800-237-9932

CONTENTS

HONORING SACRIFICE

Since June 15, 1864, Arlington National Cemetery has been the United States' most famous military cemetery. Arlington National Cemetery has a long and difficult history. More than 150 years after its founding, it has the second-largest number of burials per year of any national cemetery in the United States.

Many of the headstones at Arlington National Cemetery are laid out on a grid. They have the person's name, which branch of the military they served in, and their years of birth and death.

INSTITUTION INSIGHT

Other information that might be presented on a military headstone is the person's military rank, which war they fought in, a symbol to represent the person's religious beliefs, or what medals or special honors they received during their time of service.

This cemetery is the final resting place for more than 400,000 people, many of whom **sacrificed** their lives fighting to protect their country. Their hard work and bravery can be honored by all who visit this site. Arlington National Cemetery celebrates the lives of all who are buried there, from nurses to presidents.

FROM MEMORIAL TO HEADQUARTERS

The site of Arlington National Cemetery wasn't always a cemetery. Arlington House, which sits on the property, was built to be a memorial to President George Washington. The mansion was built by his adopted grandson, George Washington Parke Custis, and was completed in 1818.

INSTITUTION INSIGHT

Arlington House sits on top of a hill from which visitors can see Washington, D. C., and the Potomac River. Because of its location, the estate was a perfect spot from which Union soldiers could watch for Confederate troops.

Lee and his family lived at the Arlington estate when it was taken over by Union forces. Lee was married to George Washington Parke Custis's daughter, Mary Anna, who left the estate before the Union army captured it.

During the Civil War, on May 24, 1861, 3,500 Union soldiers captured the Arlington estate, which had been the home of Confederate General Robert E. Lee. The Union army began to use it as a military headquarters. The estate stood on Confederate soil in northern Virginia. Many Union soldiers lived in camps at the site. There was a special camp called Freedman's Village where many freed slaves lived and farmed.

THE NEED FOR A MILITARY CEMETERY

After Mary Anna Lee failed to pay taxes on the Arlington estate, officials put it up for sale. On January 11, 1864, the federal government bought it for $26,800 ($389,400 in today's currency).

With the amount of men dying during the Civil War increasing, cemeteries in Washington, D.C., were running out of space. Quartermaster General Montgomery Meigs, who was also a civil engineer, chose Arlington as the site of a new national cemetery. On May 13, 1864, Private William Christman of the 67th Pennsylvania Infantry became the first soldier buried in Arlington. He was only 21 years old when he died.

As part of the 150th anniversary of Arlington National Cemetery, family members placed a wreath above Private William Christman's grave. His original grave marker was just a piece of wood painted white with black lettering. He was too poor for his body to be sent back to his family for burial.

19
WM. CHRISTMAN
PA.

PROPERTY OF THE UNITED STATES

Upon General Lee's death in 1870, his son, George Washington Custis Lee, took action to regain control of the Arlington estate. He claimed that the land was illegally seized from his family and that, according to his grandfather's will, the land was rightfully his. The U.S. Supreme Court decided to return the land to him and his family in December 1882.

MONTGOMERY C. MEIGS'S GRAVE

Montgomery Meigs was a Union Army officer and a civil engineer. He had a very large role in the creation of Arlington National Cemetery.

The United States government wanted this land to remain a cemetery. Congress bought the land back from Custis Lee on March 3, 1883, for $150,000 ($3,385,890 in today's currency). Arlington would remain a final resting place for servicemen and women and their families.

NOTABLE GRAVES

Many important people are buried at Arlington National Cemetery. One of the most notable people buried at Arlington is President John F. Kennedy. Two of his children and his wife, Jacqueline Kennedy Onassis, are buried there as well.

John F. Kennedy's grave was moved in the late 1960s. The new site was thoroughly planned. The gravesite has an eternal flame and the Kennedy family chose the stones that mark the area.

INSTITUTION INSIGHT

There are three World War II prisoners of war buried in Arlington: Mario Batista (Italian), Arcangelo Prudenza (Italian), and Anton Hilberath (German). The men were held captive near the Washington, D.C., area when they died of illness.

On January 28, 1986, the seven people aboard the space shuttle *Challenger* were killed when it exploded shortly after takeoff. The astronauts have their own special memorial in Arlington. All of their names and images are on it. This monument was **dedicated** on March 21, 1987.

THE TOMB OF THE UNKNOWN SOLDIER

Sometimes when a person is killed in battle it's very hard to identify their body. This was especially difficult before **DNA** testing was invented. In order to honor soldiers who could not be identified, the United States created a memorial for them.

Four unknown U.S. soldiers from World War I were **exhumed** from their graves in France on Memorial Day in 1921. A soldier who fought in World War I chose one unknown soldier from the four, all of whom were in plain **caskets**. On November 11, 1921, the body of the Unknown Soldier was **interred** in a marble **tomb** at Arlington.

The words "Here rests in honored glory an American soldier known but to God" are written on the Tomb of the Unknown Soldier. The tomb honors all the soldiers who died in World War I but couldn't be identified.

INSTITUTION INSIGHT

Tomb Guards protect the Tomb of the Unknown Soldier 24 hours a day every day of the year.

BECOMING A TOMB GUARD

The soldiers who guard the Tomb of the Unknown Soldier are very special. To become a Tomb Guard, a soldier must be a part of the Third U.S. Infantry Regiment, or "The Old Guard." Tomb Guards have to follow strict rules. They must be completely dedicated to their training program and many soldiers who train to be a Tomb Guard fail.

INSTITUTION INSIGHT

The Tomb Guard Identification Badge is the least awarded badge in the army. It is the second least awarded badge in the U.S. military, after the Astronaut Badge.

After passing their tests, a soldier must stand guard for nine months before being awarded the Tomb Guard Identification Badge. Over 600 badges have been awarded since the late 1950s, when the badge was created.

Before they can become tomb guards, soldiers are tested on their knowledge of the job. They take exams on a **ritual** known as the Changing of the Guard, uniform preparation, and the history of the tomb.

THE CHANGING OF THE GUARD

The Changing of the Guard is performed at the Tomb of the Unknown Soldier every day of the year at specific times depending on the season. During this ritual, a relief commander walks up to the tomb and salutes it, then inspects the weapon of the new guard. The new guard and the old guard switch places.

INSTITUTION INSIGHT

Of the more than 630 people who have become Tomb Guards, there have been three female sentinels. These women must meet the same requirements as male sentinels.

The number 21 represents the 21-gun salute, which is the highest military honor that can be bestowed.

The guard marches 21 steps down a black mat in front of the tomb. He or she stops, turns to face the tomb for 21 seconds, turns to face back along the mat for 21 seconds, takes 21 steps to the other end of the mat, then repeats the process.

UNKNOWN SOLDIERS FROM OTHER WARS

Near the Tomb of the Unknown Soldier are three marble **slabs**. These are the memorials for unknown soldiers from World War II and the Vietnam and Korean Wars. The bodies of each of the unknown soldiers buried at these sites were chosen at random.

The memorial for the Vietnam War soldier is different from the others. A soldier was buried at the site in 1984. However, the soldier's identity was later revealed through DNA testing. In 1998, the remains of Air Force 1st Lieutenant Michael Joseph Blassie were exhumed and returned to his family.

LT. MICHAEL JOSEPH BLASSIE

INSTITUTION INSIGHT

It is likely that there will never be another tomb dedicated to unknown soldiers. DNA testing now allows them to be identified.

The tomb of the Vietnam War's unknown soldier will remain empty. The marble slab was changed to say "Honoring and Keeping Faith with America's Missing Servicemen 1958–1975." Blassie's remains now rest at Jefferson Barracks National Cemetery in Missouri.

THE NATION'S MOST HALLOWED GROUNDS

Arlington National Cemetery is meant to provide the friends and family members of fallen soldiers and veterans with a sense of closure. Many of those buried there are linked through their dedication and **commitment** to protecting the United States during times of war. Many sacrificed their lives in the name of the nation.

Servicemen and women from every war in U.S. history are buried in Arlington. Heroes, enemies, nationals, foreigners, freed slaves, and unknown soldiers rest in these **hallowed** grounds. This landmark is one of the most sacred places in the United States.

Arlington is dedicated to honoring those who have given their lives for their country.

GLOSSARY

casket: A coffin, or a box, in which the body of a dead person is buried.

commitment: An agreement or pledge to do something.

dedicate: To officially make something a place for honoring a person or event.

DNA: A substance that carries genetic information, located in the cells of plants and animals.

exhume: To remove a body from the place where it is buried.

hallowed: Blessed; highly respected.

inter: To bury a dead body.

ritual: An established form of a ceremony in which a series of actions are performed in a certain order.

sacrifice: The act of giving up something that you want to keep, especially in order to get or do something else or to help someone.

slab: A thick, flat piece of a hard material.

tomb: A building or chamber above or below the ground in which a dead body is kept.

INDEX

WEBSITES

Due to the changing nature of Internet links, PowerKids Press has developed an online list of websites related to the subject of this book. This site is updated regularly. Please use this link to access the list: www.powerkidslinks.com/lod/arlington